SandCastle™

Baby Mammals

It's a Baby Red Fox!

Kelly Doudna

Consulting Editor, Diane Craig, M.A./Reading Specialist

ABDO
Publishing Company

Published by ABDO Publishing Company, 8000 West 78th Street, Edina, Minnesota 55439.

Copyright © 2008 by Abdo Consulting Group, Inc. International copyrights reserved in all countries.

No part of this book may be reproduced in any form without written permission from the publisher. SandCastle™ is a trademark and logo of ABDO Publishing Company.

Printed in the United States.

Editor: Pam Price
Content Developer: Nancy Tuminelly
Cover and Interior Design and Production: Mighty Media
Photo Credits: Creatas, Digital Vision, Eyewire, Peter Arnold Inc. (BIOS Cahez Fabrice, BIOS Deschandol & Sabine Frank & Philippe, S. Muller, BIOS Cavignaux Régis, R. Siegel), Photodisc, ShutterStock

Library of Congress Cataloging-in-Publication Data

Doudna, Kelly, 1963-
 It's a baby red fox! / Kelly Doudna.
    p. cm. -- (Baby mammals)
 ISBN 978-1-60453-031-5
 1. Red fox--Infancy--Juvenile literature. I. Title.

QL737.C22D69 2008
599.775'139--dc22

                        2007038006

SandCastle™ would like to hear from you. Please send us your comments and suggestions.
sandcastle@abdopublishing.com

Vital Statistics

for the Red Fox

BABY NAME
kit, pup, cub

NUMBER IN LITTER
1 to 10, average 4 to 6

WEIGHT AT BIRTH
4 ounces

AGE OF INDEPENDENCE
10 months

ADULT WEIGHT
6 to 15 pounds

LIFE EXPECTANCY
2 to 4 years

Female red foxes are called vixens. Red fox kits have brown or gray fur when they're born.

Kits grow their red coats when they're about one month old.

Males are known as dog foxes. Dog foxes help the vixens raise their kits.

When red fox kits are about four or five weeks old, they begin to explore the world outside their dens.

Red foxes are playful. They communicate with yips, barks, whines, and howls.

Coyotes and bobcats are the main predators of red foxes. They prey mostly on red fox kits.

Red foxes have excellent senses of hearing and sight.

The twitch of an ear is all a fox needs to see its prey.

15

Foxes hunt small
mammals such as voles,
mice, and rabbits.

The fox waits for its prey
to give away its location.
Then the fox pounces.

Before kits go on real hunts, they practice with small prey that their parents take to them.

Kits stay with their parents until autumn when they are about 10 months old. Then they leave to find their own territories.

Fun Fact

About the Red Fox

Foxes are fast and agile. They can leap over obstacles as high as six and a half feet. That's taller than most people!

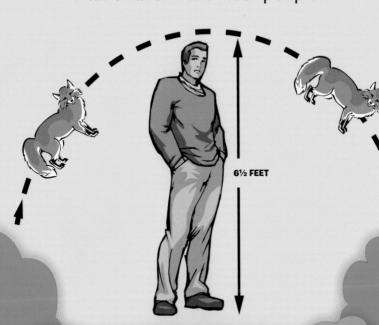

6½ FEET

Glossary

agile – able to move quickly and easily.

communicate – to share ideas, information, or feelings.

den – a small hollow used by an animal for shelter.

expectancy – an expected or likely amount.

independence – the state of no longer needing others to care for or support you.

obstacle – something that blocks progress.

predator – an animal that hunts others.

prey – 1) to hunt or catch an animal for food. 2) an animal that is hunted or caught for food.

territory – an area that is occupied and defended by an animal or a group of animals.

vole – a small rodent that is similar to a mouse, but with a shorter tail and smaller ears.